Handy Colorado Genealogy Handbook

Gary L. Morris

ISBN-13: 978-1507852712

ISBN-10: 1507852711

Table of Contents

Notes

Genealogical Research in Colorado

Colorado is rich in heritage. Many of the individuals who shaped the West came from Colorado, such as Barney Ford, the runaway slave and pioneer, Buffalo Bill Cody, and Kit Carson. The historical background of Colorado makes it especially interesting for family historians. While researching Colorado genealogy records presents a unique set of challenges; it also has its own unique rewards. There are many historical and genealogical records available for the state, and we know just where to find them. To get you started in tracing your ancestry, we'll introduce you to those records, and help you to understand:

- What they are
- Where to find them
- How to use them

These records can be found both online and off, so we'll introduce you to online websites, indexes and databases, as well as brick-and-mortar repositories and other institutions that will help with your research in Colorado. So that you will have a more comprehensive understanding of these records, we have provided a brief history of the "Centennial State" to illustrate what type of records may have been generated during specific time periods. That information will assist you in pinpointing times and locations on which to focus the search for your Colorado ancestors.

A Brief History of Colorado

The Ute Indians were Colorado's first residents, moving there from the Utah deserts. The first Europeans were Spaniards who arrived in the 16th century. In 1682 a French explorer by the name of René-Robert Cavelier claimed the area for France. The end of the French and Indian War, 1756-1763, saw the English take control until the time of the American Revolution.

The United States officially declared Colorado as its own as part of the Louisiana Purchase in 1803, and paid France 15 million dollars for the area. Additional land cessions from the Native American tribes in 1805 and 1806 saw the land open up to white settlement. Part of present day Colorado was not included in the Louisiana Purchase, but that land was eventually acquired at the end of the Mexican-American War in 1848.

When gold was discovered in 1859 more than 50,000 settlers rushed to Colorado, triggering discontent amongst the Native American peoples. Wars raged throughout the 1800's finally ending with the last battle between the plains Indians and whites in 1869 at Summit Springs. The Native Americans were settled on reservations, and Colorado was admitted to the union as the 38th State in 1876.

Important Genealogical Dates in Colorado History

1803 – Most of the area acquired in Louisiana Purchase

1848 – remainder of state acquired from Mexico

1851 – San Luis established

1858 - Gold Rush draws upwards of 50,000 settlers to the area, Denver established

1861 – Organized as US Territory

1863 - 1869 – Fierce wars fought with Cheyenne, Kiowa, Comanche, and Arapahoe Indians

1870 – Denver connected by railroad to other US cities

1876 – Statehood

1893 – Colorado women receive complete suffrage

Famous Battles Fought in Colorado

Most of the battles fought in Colorado were between the white settlers and Native Americans who inhabited the area. The battle accounts themselves can be very effective in uncovering the military records of your ancestor. They can tell you what regiments fought in which battles, and often include the names and ranks of many officers and enlisted men. Following are some of the most famous battles fought in Colorado and links to useful information about them.

Sand Creek Massacre, 1864:
http://www.pbs.org/weta/thewest/resources/archives/four/sandcrk.htm

Battle of Beecher Island, 1868:
http://www.legendsofamerica.com/co-beecherisland.html

Battle of Summit Springs, 1869:
http://public.fotki.com/jcocktail/summit-springs-batt/

Meeker Massacre, 1879: http://www.legendsofamerica.com/na-indianwarbattles-2.html

Common Colorado Genealogical Issues and Resources to Overcome Them

Boundary Changes: Boundary changes are a common obstacle when researching Colorado ancestors. You could be searching for an ancestor's record in one county when in fact it is stored in a different one due to historical county boundary changes. The **Atlas of Historical County Boundaries** can help you to overcome that problem. It provides a chronological listing of every boundary change that has occurred in the history of Colorado.

Atlas of Historical County Boundaries:
http://publications.newberry.org/ahcbp/documents/CO_Consolidated _Chronology.htm#Consolidated_Chronology

Name Changes: Surname changes, variations, and misspellings can complicate genealogical research. It is important to check all spelling variations. Soundex, a program that indexes names by sound, is a useful first step, but you can't rely on it completely as some name variations result in different Soundex codes. The surnames could be different, but the first name may be different too. You can also find records filed under initials, middle names, and nicknames as well, so you will need to **get creative with surname variations** and spellings in order to cover all the possibilities. For help with surname variations read our instructional article on **How to Use Soundex**.

get creative with surname variations:
http://obituarieshelp.org/blog/?p=634

How to Use Soundex: http://obituarieshelp.org/blog/?p=505

Colorado Genealogical Organizations and Archives

Genealogical resources include not only records, but the organizations that house them, or can direct you to them. These institutions include: *Archives, Libraries, Genealogical Societies, Family History Centers, Universities, Churches, and Museums.*

Following are links to their websites, their physical addresses, and a summary of the records you can find there.

Colorado Archives

Colorado State Archives – census schedules, vital records post-1900, military records, court records, city directories

1313 Sherman, Room 1B20
Denver, CO 80203
Tel: 303-866-2358
Fax: 303-866-2229

Colorado State Archives:
http://www.colorado.gov/dpa/doit/archives/geneal.htm

Denver Public Library – pioneer records, military records, death records, railroad records, city directories

Denver Public Library
10 W. 14th Avenue Parkway
Denver, CO 80204-2731
Tel:: 720-865-1821
Fax: 720-865-1880

Denver Public Library:
http://history.denverlibrary.org/research/genealogy.html

Arthur Lakes Library (Colorado School of Mines) – mining history, historical photos, maps

1400 Illinois Street
Golden, CO 80401
Tel: 303-273-3911
Fax: 303-273-3199
Arthur Lakes Library: http://library.mines.edu/

Ira J. Taylor Library (Iliff School of Technology) – Multi-denominational religious records

2201 South University Boulevard
Denver, Colorado 80210
Tel: 303-744-1287
Fax : 303-777-0164
Ira J. Taylor Library: http://www.iliff.edu/

Auraria Library, University of Colorado at Denver - manuscript collections, historical records

1100 Lawrence Street
Denver, CO 80204
Tel: 303-556-2740
Auraria Library: http://archives.auraria.edu/

Norlin Library (Special Collections), University of Colorado at Boulder – manuscript collection, historical photos, maps, rare books, historical records

University Libraries
184 UCB, 1720 Pleasant Street
University of Colorado
Boulder, CO 80309-0184
Tel: 303-492-6144, 303-492-7521
Norlin Library (Special Collections):
http://ucblibraries.colorado.edu/specialcollections/index.htm

Colorado Genealogical and Historical Societies

Genealogical and historical societies have access to extensive catalogues of genealogical data. They are also able to offer expert guidance for genealogical researchers. Many members are professional genealogists who are most willing to share their expertise in finding ancestors.

Colorado Genealogical Society - Assists and supports family historians in Colorado including researchers, libraries, and archives.

Colorado Genealogical Society
P.O. Box 9218
Denver, CO 80209-0218
Email: info@cogensoc.us

Colorado Genealogical Society: http://www.cogensoc.us/

Colorado Historical Society - Stephen H. Hart Research Library - Books, maps, architectural drawings, family albums, photographic prints, magazines and newspapers, and many more historical resources.

History Colorado
1200 Broadway
Denver, CO 80203
Tel: 303-447-8679

Colorado Historical Society: http://www.historycolorado.org/

Colorado Society of Hispanic Genealogy – quarterly journal and information on various subjects geared to the beginner and advanced genealogical researcher or family historian.

2300 South Patton Court
Denver, CO 80219-5212

Colorado Society of Hispanic Genealogy:
http://www.hispanicgen.org/index.html

Ira M. Beck Memorial Archives - Rocky Mountain Jewish Historical Society – historical record of the Jews.

University of Denver
Sturm Hall
2000 E. Asbury Ave, Room 157
Denver, CO 80208-0911
Phone: 303-871-3016
Fax: 303-871-3037
Email: jeanne.abrams@du.edu

Ira M. Beck Memorial Archives :
http://www.du.edu/ahss/cjs/rmjhs/archives/

Colorado Family History Centers

The Family History Centers run by the LDS Church offer free access to billions of genealogical records for free to the general public. They also provide classes on genealogy and one-on-one assistance to inexperienced family historians. Here you will find a **Complete Listing of Colorado Family History Centers**.

Complete Listing of Colorado Family History Centers:
https://familysearch.org/locations/centerlocator

Additional Colorado Genealogical Resources

Colorado Mailing Lists

Mailing lists are internet based facilities that use email to distribute a single message to all who subscribe to it. When information on a particular surname, new records, or any other important genealogy information related to the mailing list topic becomes available, the subscribers are alerted to it. Joining a mailing list is an excellent way to stay up to date on Colorado genealogy research topics. Rootsweb have an extensive listing of **Colorado Mailing Lists** on a variety of topics.

Colorado Mailing Lists:
http://lists.rootsweb.ancestry.com/index/usa/CO/misc.html

Colorado Message Boards

A message board is another internet based facility where people can post questions about a specific genealogy topic and have it answered by other genealogists. If you have questions about a surname, record type, or research topic, you can post your question and other researchers and genealogists will help you with the answer. Be sure to check back regularly, as the answers are not emailed to you. The Colorado message boards at **Rootsweb** are completely free to use.

Rootsweb:
http://boards.rootsweb.com/localities.northam.usa.states/mb.ashx

Colorado Newspapers and Periodicals

Many genealogy periodicals and historical newspapers contain reprinted copies of family genealogies, transcripts of family Bible records, information about local records and archives, census indexes, church records, queries, land records, obituaries, court records, cemetery records, and wills. The following sites have historical Colorado newspapers and periodicals that you can search online or on-site.

Denver Public Library – massive collection of historical newspapers and magazines dating from 1849

Denver Public Library:
http://www.history.denverlibrary.org/collections/newspapers_description.html

Tutt Library, Colorado College – full text newspapers and American periodicals dating from the early 18th century. Includes African American and Civil War Newspapers, special interest magazines, literary journals, women's and children's magazines, and many other historically-significant periodicals

Tutt Library
1021 North Cascade Avenue
Colorado Springs, CO 80903-3252
Tel: 719 389-6662

Tutt Library:
http://www2.coloradocollege.edu/library/index.php/collections/history-databases

NewspaperArchive.com – largest online database of historical newspapers in the world.

NewspaperArchive.com: http://newspaperarchive.com/

Historical Colorado Maps and Gazetteers

Maps are an integral part of genealogical research. They help us to
locate landmarks, towns, cities, parishes, states, provinces,
waterways and roads and streets. They also help us to determine
when and where boundary changes might have taken place, and give
us a visualization of the area we're researching in. For locating place
names, a gazetteer is the best possible resource for any genealogist.
Gazetteers are also sometimes called "place name dictionaries", and
can help you to locate the area in which you need to conduct
research. Below are links to the maps and gazetteers for research in
Colorado.

Peabody GNIS Service – Colorado:
http://peabody.research.yale.edu/cgi-
bin/Query.GNIS?ST=Colorado&SU=1

Color Landform Atlas – Colorado:
http://fermi.jhuapl.edu/states/co_0.html

1985 U.S. Atlas: http://www.livgenmi.com/1895/CO/

Colorado Hometown Locator:
http://colorado.hometownlocator.com/

Colorado City Directories

City directories are similar to telephone directories in that they list the residents of a particular area. The difference though is what is important to genealogists, and that is they pre-date telephone directories. You can find an ancestor's information such as their street address, place of employment, occupation, or the name of their spouse. A one-stop-shop for finding city directories in Colorado is the **Colorado Online Historical Directories** which contains a listing of every available city and historical directory related to Colorado.

Colorado Online Historical Directories:
https://sites.google.com/site/onlinedirectorysite/Home/usa/co

Pikes Peak Library District - Colorado Springs City Directories: 1879 - 1922

Pikes Peak Library District
P.O. Box 1579
Colorado Springs, CO 80901
(719) 531-6333

Pikes Peak Library District: http://ppld.org/colorado-springs-city-directories-1879-1922

Fort Collins History Connection - Online database of over 100 Fort Collins and Larimer County directories dating from 1902 to 2005

Fort Collins History Connection:
http://history.fcgov.com/archive/directories.php

Colorado Genealogical Records

Birth, Death, Marriage and Divorce Records – Birth, death, and marriage records are the most basic, yet most important records attached to your ancestor. They are generally referred to as vital records as they record vital life events. The reason for their importance is that they not only place your ancestor in a specific place at a definite time, but potentially connect the individual to other relatives. Below is a list of repositories and websites where you can find Colorado vital records

Colorado Center for Health and Environmental Information and Statistics – birth, death, marriage, civil union, and divorce records

Colorado Department of Public Health and Environment
Vital Records Section
4300 Cherry Creek Drive South
HSVRD-VR-A1
Denver, CO 80246-1530
Tel: (303) 692-2200
Email: vital.records@state.co.us

Colorado Center for Health and Environmental Information and Statistics: http://www.colorado.gov/cs/Satellite/CDPHE-CHEIS/CBON/1251593016787

Colorado State Archives - 3,000 Colorado births from 1863-1899 on microfilm, death index for Denver, 1872-1909, marriage indexes

1313 Sherman, Room 1B20
Denver, CO 80203
Tel: 303-866-2358
Fax: 303-866-2229

Colorado State Archives:
http://www.colorado.gov/dpa/doit/archives/geneal.htm

Gilpin County Brides' And Groom's Marriage Index 1864-1944
– transcription of marriage index from Gilpin County during years stated

Gilpin County Brides' And Groom's Marriage Index 1864-1944
link to:
http://www.colorado.gov/dpa/doit/archives/marriage/gilpin_index.ht
m

Marriages of Grand County, Colorado – marriage index for Grand County covering the years 1874-1974

Marriages of Grand County, Colorado link to:
http://www.wargo.org/grandcomarriages.htm

Census Reports

Census records are among the most important genealogical documents for placing your ancestor in a particular place at a specific time. Like BDM records, they can also lead you to other ancestors, particularly those who were living under the authority of the head of household.

Colorado census records exist from 1850 -1940 and many images and indexes can be viewed online. Following are the best places to find Colorado census records.

Colorado State Archives – census records from 1850 - 1880 and 1900 - 1920, the special 1885 Colorado State Census and the special Indian Census (1885-1944)

1313 Sherman
Room 1B20
Denver
CO 80203
Tel: 303-866-2358
Fax: 303-866-2229

Colorado State Archives link to:
http://www.colorado.gov/dpa/doit/archives/census.html

U.S National Archives – Federal census records on microfilm available from 1790 to 1940.

U.S National Archives: http://www.archives.gov/research/census/

Family Link – Colorado census records from 1870-1940

Family Link link to:
http://www.familylink.com/contentview.aspx?p=co

Colorado Church Records

Church and synagogue records are a valuable resource, especially for baptisms, marriages, and burials that took place before 1900. You will need to at least have an idea of your ancestor's religious denomination, and in most cases you will have to visit a brick and mortar establishment to view them.

Most church records are kept by the individual church, although in some denominations, records are placed in a regional archive or maintained at the diocesan level. Local Historical Societies are sometimes the repository for the state's older church records. Below are links archives that maintain church records, as well as a few databases that can be viewed online.

The **Family History Library** contains many church records from a variety of denominations on microfilm. and microfiche.

Family History Library:
http://familysearch.org/learn/wiki/en/Family_History_Library

Central depositories for Denominational Records

Episcopal

Diocese of Colorado
1300 Washington St
Denver, CO 80203-2008
Tel: (303) 837-1173
Diocese of Colorado link to:http://www.coloradodiocese.org/

Methodist

Ira J. Taylor Library (Iliff School of Technology)
2201 South University Boulevard
Denver, Colorado 80210
Tel: 303-744-1287
Fax : 303-777-0164
Ira J. Taylor Library: http://www.iliff.edu/

Presbyterian

Presbyterian Historical Society
425 Lombard Street
Philadelphia, PA 19147
Tel: (215) 627-1852
Fax: (215) 627-0509
refdesk@history.pcusa.org

Presbyterian Historical Society: http://www.history.pcusa.org/

Roman Catholic

Archives of the Diocese of Colorado Springs
228 North Cascade Ave.
Colorado Springs, CO 80903
Tel: (719) 636-2345

Archives of the Diocese of Colorado Springs link to:
http://www.diocs.org/
Archives of the Archdiocese of Denver
1300 South Steele St.
Denver, CO 80210-2599
Tel: (303) 722-4687
Fax: (303) 331-8071

Archives of the Archdiocese of Denver : http://www.archden.org/

Colorado Military Records

More than 40 million Americans have participated in some time of war service since America was colonized. The chance of finding your ancestor amongst those records is exceptionally high. Military records can even reveal individuals who never actually served, such as those who registered for the two World Wars but were never called to duty.

Below are a number of links to websites and archives that contain Colorado military records.

Colorado State Archives - civil war records, Colorado Volunteers index 1861-1865, WWI enlistments, War Risk Insurance applicants list, Spanish American War records, Rosters and Muster Rolls 1861-1921, Service Records 1861-1946, Aadministrative Files of the Adjutant General 1862-1950, Annual/Biennial Reports of the Adjutant General 1867-1983, Special and General Orders 1864-1986, Governor's Guard Record Book 1862-1863, Military Occupation of the Coal Strike Zone of Colorado by the National Guard 1913-1914, Misc. Veterans Rosters 1893-1946

Colorado State Archives:
http://www.colorado.gov/dpa/doit/archives/military.html

U.S. National Archives – WWI Draft registration cards, casualties lists, WWI and WWII service records, Korean War records, Vietnam War records, Civil War and Spanish-American War records, and casualties lists.

U.S. National Archives:
http://www.archives.gov/research/military/veterans/online.html

US Department of Veterans Affairs Nationwide Gravesite Locator – includes information on veterans and their family members buried in veterans and military cemeteries having a government grave marker.

US Department of Veterans Affairs Nationwide Gravesite Locator: http://gravelocator.cem.va.gov/

United States Index to Indian Wars Pension Files, 1892-1926 – military pension records of soldiers who fought in the Indian Wars between 1817 and 1898

United States Index to Indian Wars Pension Files, 1892-1926:: https://familysearch.org/search/collection/1979427

Civil War Soldiers Service Records - Service records for both Union and Confederate soldiers indexed by soldier's name, rank, and unit.

Civil War Soldier Service Records: http://go.fold3.com/civilwar_records/

Colorado Cemetery Records

As convenient as it is to search cemetery records online, keep in mind that there are a few disadvantages over visiting a cemetery in person. They are:

- Tombstone information is not always accurately transcribed
- The arrangement of the graves in a cemetery can be crucial as family members are often buried next to each other or in the same grave. This arrangement is not always preserved in the alphabetical indexes that are found online.

With that information in mind, the following websites have databases that can be searched online for Colorado Cemetery records.

Colorado Tombstone Transcription Project - death and burial records

Colorado Tombstone Transcription Project:
http://www.usgwtombstones.org/colorado/colorado.html

African American Cemeteries Online – African American, slave, and Native American cemetery records

African American Cemeteries Online:
http://africanamericancemeteries.com/

Access Genealogy – huge database of Colorado cemetery record transcriptions

Access Genealogy:
http://www.accessgenealogy.com/cemetery/colorado.htm

Find a Grave – over 100 million grave records can be searched on this site. Search can be conducted by name, location, or cemetery name.

Find a Grave: http://www.findagrave.com/

Interment.net - A free online database containing approximately 4 million cemetery records from around the world.

Interment.net: http://www.interment.net/

Billion Graves – as the name implies, you can search a billion records including headstone photos, transcriptions, cemetery records, and grave locations.

Billion Graves:
http://billiongraves.com/pages/search/index.php#cemetery

Colorado Obituaries

Obituaries can reveal a wealth about our ancestor and other relatives. You can search our **Colorado Newspaper Obituaries Listings** from hundreds of Colorado newspapers online for free.

Colorado Newspaper Obituaries Listings:
http://obituarieshelp.org/colorado_newspaper_obituaries.html

Colorado Wills and Probate Records

The documents found in a probate packet may include a complete inventory of a person's estate, newspaper entries, witness testimony, a copy of a will, list of debtors and creditors, names of executors or trustees, names of heirs. They can not only tell you about the ancestor you're currently researching, but lead to other ancestors. Most of these records must be accessed at a county court or clerk's office, but some can be found online as well. You can obtain copies of the original probate records by writing to the county clerk.

Colorado County Clerks Roster:
http://www.sos.state.co.us/pubs/elections/Resources/files/CountyCle rkRosterWebsite.pdf

Colorado State Archives – probate records from many Colorado counties dating from 1870-1964, wills, tax inheritance records

Colorado State Archives:
http://www.colorado.gov/dpa/doit/archives/hrd/HRD.htm

Denver Probate Court – probate records for Denver County only

Denver Probate Court:
http://www.courts.state.co.us/Courts/Denver_Probate/Records.cfm

Colorado Immigration and Naturalization Records

The naturalization process generated many types of records, including petitions, declarations of intention, and oaths of allegiance. These records can provide family historians with information such as a person's birth date and place of birth, immigration year, marital status, spouse information, occupation, witnesses' names and addresses, and more.

Colorado State Archives - naturalization records for the majority of counties in Colorado including: final documents, petitions, certificates of naturalization stub books, repatriations, and declarations of intent.

Colorado State Archives:
http://www.colorado.gov/dpa/doit/archives/natural.html

The **Colorado Genealogical Society** possesses abstracts of some naturalization records and they have been published in their periodical *The Colorado Genealogist*

Colorado Genealogical Society: http://www.cogensoc.us/

The **Foothills Genealogical Society** has Naturalization indexes for Clear Creek County and a Declaration of intents index for the Denver area.

Foothills Genealogical Society:
http://foothillsgenealogy.org/cpage.php?pt=24

The **Denver Public Library** - Denver and Pueblo Naturalization index for the years 1877-1952; naturalization records index for Park County

Denver Public Library:
http://digital.denverlibrary.org/cdm/compoundobject/collection/p160
79coll7/id/1284/rec/1

Archive Aspen possesses a Naturalization records index for Pitkin County for the years 1888-1908

Archive Aspen link to: http://www.archiveaspen.org/historic-directories-records.htm

Colorado Railway Records

Railroads played an important role in the settlement of Colorado, bringing in many settlers from the east and as far away as Mexico. The records of railway employees can be a valuable genealogical source, especially if your ancestor was a railway employee. Following are places both online and off where you can search railway records for Colorado ancestors.

Denver Public Library – Railway employee records, maps, manuscripts, periodicals, pension records and more from a large number of railway companies serving Colorado

Denver Public Library:
http://digital.denverlibrary.org/cdm/compoundobject/collection/p160 79coll23/id/391/rec/1

Colorado Railroad Museum – employee records and historical accounts of many railway companies including Union Pacific, Atchison, Topeka and Santa Fe Railroad, Colorado & Southern Railway Co., Denver, Leadville & Gunnison Railway Co., Denver and Rio Grande Western Railroad Company, and the Chicago Burlington and Quincy Railroad.

17155 W. 44th Avenue,
Golden, CO 80403
Tel: 303-279-4591, 800-365-6263
Email: via online contact form

Colorado Railroad Museum: http://coloradorailroadmuseum.org/

Native American Records

Access Genealogy – Native American census records, tribal histories, and much more

Access Genealogy: http://www.accessgenealogy.com/native/

Midwest Genealogy Center – a wide variety of records from the vast majority of Native American tribes in the United States on microfilm

Midwest Genealogy Center
3440 S. Lee's Summit Road
Independence, Missouri

Midwest Genealogy Center:
http://www.mymcpl.org/_uploaded_resources/MGC-micronatamer.pdf

The **National Archives** - information about American Indians who maintained their ties to Federally-recognized Tribes (1830-1970).

National Archives link: http://www.archives.gov/research/native-americans/

Bureau of Indian Affairs: http://www.bia.gov/

American Indians Records Repository - records dating from the 1700s including trust, education and other historic Indian Affairs records

American Indian Records Repository
Meritex Enterprises
17501 West 98th Street
Lenexa, KS 66219
Phone: 913-888-0601

American Indians Records Repository:
http://www.doi.gov/ost/records_mgmt/american-indian-records-repository.cfm

Missing Matriarchs – Resources for Researching Female Colorado Ancestors

Looking for female ancestors requires an adjustment of how we view traditional records sources. A woman's identity was often under that of her husband, and often individual records for them can be difficult to locate. The following resources are effective in locating female ancestors in Colorado where traditional records may not reveal them.

Marriage and Divorce Records

Marriage records have been recorded by the county clerk and recorders offices since 1861. Divorces were overseen by the County district courts since the creation of counties. The **Family History Library** has a few county records for Colorado on microfilm such as:

- Denver County Clerk marriage extracts, 1849-1880 (film 0928067) also at the Denver County Courthouse in Denver, CO.
- Arapahoe County Recorder of Deeds records (contains some marriage certificates), 1860-1934 (film 1954194) also at the Colorado State Archives in Denver, CO.

The **Boulder Genealogical Society** has Boulder County marriage records from 1860-1900 that can be viewed online.

Family History Library:
https://familysearch.org/locations/saltlakecity-library

Boulder Genealogical Society:
http://homepages.rootsweb.ancestry.com/~bldrco/bcmarriages/home.html

Bibliographies

1. *A Lady's Life in the Rocky Mountains,* Isabella Bird (Ballantine Books, 1960)
2. *One Hundred Years of Colorado Women,* Elinor Bluemel (The Author, 1973)
3. *The Sand Creek Massacre,* Stan Hoig (University of Oklahoma Press, 1961)
4. *Hispanic Families of New Mexico and Southern Colorado, 1538-1990,* Donald Mulligan (University of New Mexico Press, 1990)
5. *The Magnificent Mountain Women: Adventures in the Colorado Rockies,* Janet Robertson (University of Nebraska Press, 1991)

Selected Resources for Colorado Women's History

Colorado Coalition for Women's History
PO Box 673
1200 Madison
Denver, CO 80206

Women of the West Museum
4001 Discovery Drive
Boulder, CO 80303-7816

Western Historical Collection
University of Colorado
Boulder, CO 80309

Common Colorado Surnames

The following surnames are among the most common in Colorado. The list is by no means exhaustive. If your surname doesn't appear in the list it doesn't mean that you have no Colorado connections, only that your surname may be less common.

Abrams, Anghern, Barlow, Black, Bogue, Booco, Buchholz, Bureman, Burns, Caddy, Case, Chipperfield, Clark, Cody, Cowden, Curry, DoBois, DaLee, DeSousa, Doll, Doyle, Eldred, Elliot, Fahey, Ferguson, Flannery, Forster, French, Gilmer, Gomez, Greenleaf, Greiner, Griffith, Hall, Hammer, Harlan, Herwick, Hohstadt, Hooper, Horn, Hunter, Jones, Kinney, Kramer, Lane, Lemon, Love, Mather, McGlochlin, McPhee, Moore, Neal, Noble, Pallister, Pando, Phillips, Rabedew, Ray, Reynolds, Rochford, Rogers, Ruder, Rule, Rundell, Savage, Schulz, Scott, Sheward, Shippee, Shute, Sifers, Sloss, Smith, Strobridge, Terrell, Thoborg, Tourville, Wilds, Willison, Yost, Young, Zalar, Zimmerman

About the Author

Gary L. Morris worked from 2009 to 2014 as a professional researcher for a major player in the genealogy field. After tracing his family lineage back to 1683, he found that genealogy could be an expensive undertaking. As such, has decided to publish these helpful guides to share the valuable free information he has discovered during his career to help others trace their family lineages as inexpensively as possible. An avid genealogist himself, he hopes you will find this guide factual, thorough, helpful, and most of all, effective in helping you to find your family members.

Notes

Notes

www.ingramcontent.com/pod-product-compliance
Lightning Source LLC
Chambersburg PA
CBHW070516290526
45790CB00003B/1241